SCHOLAST

20 Reading *and* Writing Centers

Fun Literacy-Building Centers With Ready-to-Use Picture Cards, Word Cards, Templates, Game Boards, and More

by Rosalie Franzese

New York • Toronto • London • Auckland • Sydney
Mexico City • New Delhi • Hong Kong • Buenos Aires **Teaching** *Resources*

Dedication

To my beautiful little girl, Mary

Acknowledgments

I would like to thank Ivan Kushner, principal of PS 19, for his enthusiastic support of this work.

I would also like to thank Debbie Rosen, a wonderful teacher who provided me with photographs of her classroom and who continues to bring the joy of literacy to her kindergarten students.

Abby Miller, an outstanding teacher who believes in the magic of centers in her classroom.

Thanks to Lindsay Golden for implementing the literacy program in her kindergarten classroom.

Finally, to Joanna Davis-Swing, my editor, for her insight, understanding, and flexibility for bringing this work to print.

Cover design by Brian LaRossa
Cover illustrations by Shelly Dieterichs
Interior design by Sarah Morrow
Illustrations on pages 12–13 by Yvette Banek
Illustrations on pages 54–58 by Richard Kolding
Other illustrations by Rusty Fletcher, James Hale, Ellen Matlach Hassell,
Mike Moran, Sarah Morrow, Brenda Sexton, and Karen Sevaly

3 4 5 6 7 8 9 10   40   11 10 09 08 07

Contents

Introduction

Through the years I have found that center time is the highlight of a kindergartner's day. Every day the children look forward to working—or, as they experience it, "playing"—at centers. I watch them enter the classroom and go directly to the center board to find where they'll be working. I notice a buzz of excitement and delight in the room when children notice a new station icon on the board. I am convinced that center time is fun, yet purposeful, a very important component of helping children become readers and writers.

These Reading Play Stations, as I call them, or literacy center activities, engage children in playful, game-like activities that involve rereading familiar texts, practicing reading and writing strategies, developing letter-sound correspondence, and practicing other word study skills. This kind of meaningful and purposeful play comes out of shared reading, when the whole class reads enlarged pieces of texts while the teacher models strategies; word study, which helps children understand how letters and words work; and shared and interactive writing lessons, when early writing strategies are demonstrated. Reading Play Stations give children the opportunity to practice skills they're learning during these lessons and provides them with the support they need to become independent readers.

Each station includes one focused activity that may have one or more steps. I introduce the stations and model their use during the first six weeks of school before we begin guided reading. When I begin guided reading, the children I'm not meeting with work at stations independently or in groups of two or three. At any one time I may have as many as eight stations running. Children simply gather the necessary materials stored in specific areas of the room, group their chairs together, or find places on the carpet to work together at the stations.

Introducing Reading Play Stations to the Class

Reading Play Stations require a great deal of whole-class modeling before children can use them independently. It's important to introduce them gradually, one or two each day, so children aren't overwhelmed. Children need to master a couple of stations at a time before opening up others.

Because many children will be doing a variety of simultaneous activities that involve verbalization, we begin by discussing how important it is to use "inside" voices when working at reading stations. I demonstrate every station activity to the whole class at the same time. I'll often model the procedure by thinking aloud and saying the steps as I do them. I also have some children model how to work in a station while the others look on. We then discuss the class's observations. During this modeling time, students learn how to get the materials for stations, set them up, and put them away.

After stations are up and running and before guided reading begins, I walk around and monitor children as they work. After station time, we always discuss the positive things that happened as well as what we still need to work on. Possible discussion topics include procedures, finishing one station game before moving on to another, working quietly and cooperatively, taking turns, or cleaning up stations. By the time guided reading begins six weeks into the school year, students are generally comfortable working in stations.

Managing Reading Play Stations

I use a Reading Play Station Schedule Chart to show students what stations they'll be working on. There are many ways to set up a reading station chart. Just be sure your system is simple and clear so that children are confident as they move around the room from station to station.

One of my station charts uses a "house" theme and is color-coded. For each group of five or six children, I make a different-colored house (pink, red, orange, yellow, and green). I attach the names of the children in a specific group to the roof of the house with Velcro. The composition of children working in station groups usually matches that of the guided reading groups, once they are established.

I also provide opportunities for children to work with other children besides the ones in their reading group. Before guided reading groups are established, I pair children with a variety of different students to help them feel comfortable working at the stations. I assign each child a partner by placing the two names side by side on the roof of the house on the Reading Station Schedule Chart. I also make station icons, on which I write the name of the station and draw a picture of the station. I put three of these inside the house below the names, with the first icon corresponding to the first pair of children, the second icon to the second pair, and so on. I decide which students will go to which stations, based on their individual needs. Once children have finished at their initial assigned station, they can go to any of the other two stations in their house, if the other children have finished working in them.

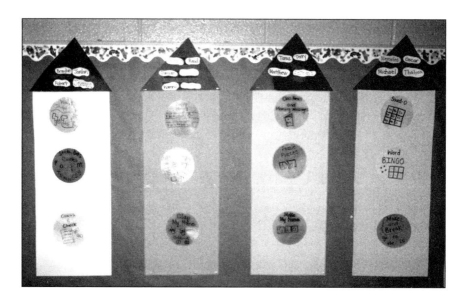

Another way to set up a station chart is to use a pocket chart. Put the station icons on the left side of the chart and the names of two children to the right. The children find their names on the chart and go to the stations indicated by the icon. There are many ways to set up these kinds of charts. They need to be clearly presented in a manner that children can understand and work with.

Station Materials

Each station has its own bin, basket, or plastic bag labeled with the same icon used for the Reading Play Station Schedule Chart. I keep all the stations in a specific area in the classroom where children have easy access to them. Many of the stations require magnetic letters, boards, and plastic sorting trays. You'll need several sets of upper- and lower-case letters and some sorting trays, each of which contains separate compartments. It's important to store the letters with several of the same letter (mixing upper and lower case) in each compartment so that children don't have to spend time searching for letters. Other materials frequently used in reading stations include index cards, dry-erase markers, letter picture cards, alphabet charts, and plastic baggies.

Managing Tips

- Always demonstrate a station before having the children work with it.

- Organize materials so that they are readily available and accessible.

- Establish comfortable routines and systems that allow the children to work independently.

- Match children with stations that support their needs.

- Occasionally, have students choose the station they want to work on.

- Take away stations that students have mastered.

- Always keep stations updated.

- When creating a station, think about the purpose behind each activity.

- Have students reread familiar texts if they finish all station work.

Making Changes

I continually update the play stations and develop new activities as the need arises. I make minor adjustments, such as incorporating information from a new Big Book or poem or new high-frequency words into existing stations. If children no longer need practice with a specific skill, I take away the station that reinforces that skill. If I notice that students need more help with mastering a specific skill, I create a new station for it.

I make sure to send children to the specific stations that meet their individual needs.

Bibliography

Cunningham, P. (2000). *Phonics they use.* New York: Addison Wesley Longman.

Cunningham, P., Allington, R. (1999). *Classrooms that work: They can all read and write.* New York: Addison Wesley Longman.

Franzese, R. (2002). *Reading and writing in kindergarten: A practical guide.* New York: Scholastic.

Snowball, D., and Bolton, F. (1999). *Spelling K–8: Planning and teaching.* Portland, ME: Stenhouse.

CHAPTER 1

Phonemic Awareness and Phonics

The centers in this section help students hear and identify sounds in words, in order to build their phonemic awareness. Other centers provide practice in letter-sound correspondence, or phonics. Both phonemic awareness and phonics are key skills for beginning readers and writers. These centers make practice with sounds and letters fun and meaningful, providing a solid foundation for young students to build on.

Station 1: Say My Name and Match the Sound

To use at the beginning of the year

Skills Practiced
- Developing letter-sound correspondence (initial letters)
- Reading high-frequency words (names of classmates)

Preparation

1. Make a set of class name cards by writing each child's name on a separate index card. Underline the first letter of each name.

2. Make a separate set of 26 picture cards, each one representing a letter of the alphabet. Use the cards provided on pages 12–13 or create your own from photos in magazines, old unusable books, alphabet poster charts, and alphabet matching games.

3. To make picture cards, cut out a picture and glue it on an index card. On the back of the card, write the word that corresponds to the picture and underline its initial letter.

4. Place the two sets of cards in labeled plastic bags: Picture Cards and Name Cards. Label a basket or box "Say My Name and Match the Sound" and then model the procedure described below before establishing the center.

> **Materials**
>
> Index cards
>
> Picture cards (see pages 12–13 for an alphabet set)

How to Play

1. Place the class set of names face up in a row on a flat surface.
2. Choose a picture card and think about the specific letter that the picture begins with.
3. Match the picture card to the appropriate name card that has the same initial letter. For example, if a player picks up a picture of a cat, he or she would place it next to the name Carl.
4. Match the other picture cards to the appropriate name cards.
5. If a picture card does not match any of the names, place that picture card aside.

Note: Make sure you have a picture card for every child's name. For example, if child's name is <u>Sh</u>antel *have a picture of a* <u>sh</u>ell.

Station 2: Sound-O

To use at the beginning and middle of the year

Skills Practiced
- Developing letter-sound correspondence (initial letters)

Preparation

1. Make a game board using the template on pages 14–15. Laminate it if desired.
2. Prepare 26 picture cards, each showing an item beginning with a different letter. You can use the pictures on pages 16 and 17, or you can prepare your own. Paste the pictures on index cards and trim them to match the size of the squares on the game board. Write the name of the object on the back of its card and underline its initial letter.
3. Place the game board and picture cards in a basket labeled "Sound-O." Model the procedure below before making the center available to students.

Materials

Picture cards (see pages 16–17 for an alphabet set) with the name of the picture printed on the back

A game board divided; see template on pages 14–15.

How to Play

1. Pick up a picture card, say the name of the object aloud, and place it on the letter that corresponds to the initial sound of the object.
2. Continue until all the letters on the game board are covered.
3. Remove the cards, checking each one against the word on the back.

Station 3: Picture-Sound Match

To use at the beginning and middle of the year

Skills practiced
- Developing letter-sound correspondence

Preparation

1. Use the template on page 18 to create the Picture-Sound Match boards on heavy card stock or cardboard.

2. Choose three pictures; each should start with a different letter. Glue them on the left-hand side of the card, one picture in each of the three sections.

3. On the right side of the card, write (in random order) the letters that correspond to the initial sound of the pictures shown, one letter in each section. Laminate the card. (See sample at right.)

4. Place the Picture-Sound Match boards and markers in a basket labeled "Picture-Sound Match." Model the procedure below before making the center available to students.

How to Play

Match the pictures to their appropriate initial letters by using an erasable marker to draw connecting lines.

Variation

Set up the game so that pictures and letters represent ending consonant sounds.

Materials

Laminated Picture-Sound Match boards (see template on page 18)

• Heavy card stock or cardboard

• Pictures (use pictures on pages 12–13 or 16–17 or your own)

Dry-erase markers

Station 4: Rhyming and Chunking

To use at the beginning of the year

Skills Practiced

• Hearing similar sounds in different words
• Understanding that words that rhyme or sound the same usually have the same chunks

Preparation

1. Create up to ten sets of picture cards by putting a picture on the front of the card and the corresponding word for it with the chunk highlighted on the back. (See pages 19–20 for nine pairs of rhyming word picture cards.) For example, if the picture were a *goat* the *oat* chunk would be highlighted on the back of the card. Make another picture card with a different picture and word. This word has to have the same chunk as its pair. For example, a picture of a boat would be the match for *goat*. Each card will match with another card in which the picture and word is different but the chunk is the same.

2. Place the picture cards in a basket labeled "Rhyming and Chunking." Model the procedure below before making the center available to students.

Materials

Rhyming picture cards

• Pictures of words that have the same chunk; see samples on pages 19–20

Index cards

How to Play

1. Spread out the cards with the pictures face up.
2. Pick up a picture card and say the word (for example, "goat").
3. Find another picture card that rhymes with the card that was just chosen and say the word (for example, "boat").
4. Turn both cards over and check to see if the chunks match.
5. Put the rhyming pair on the side.

Station 5: Let's Highlight!

To use at the middle and end of the year

Skills Practiced

- Identifying, articulating, and isolating beginnings and endings of words

Preparation

1. Make two sets of different picture cards, one for beginning sounds and one for ending sounds. You can use the pictures on pages 12–13 or 16–17 for initial sounds. You can use the picture cards on page 21 for ending sounds. Mount the pictures on index cards or card stock, leaving room at the bottom to write the beginning or ending sounds.

2. Under each picture in both sets, list three choices of beginning or ending sounds. For example, if the card has a picture of a dog on it and you're teaching ending sounds, the choices might be *k*, *j*, and *g*; see sample at right.

3. Write the word for each object on the backs of the cards. Underline the beginning sounds of the objects for one set of cards and underline the ending sounds of the objects in the second set of cards.

4. Place the picture cards in separate baskets labeled "Let's Highlight: Initial Sounds" and "Let's Highlight: Ending Sounds." Model the procedure below before making the center available to students. Use only one basket at a time to avoid confusion.

Materials

Picture cards (see page 21)
- Cardboard paper or index cards
- Pictures of various objects (see pages 12–13, 16–17, and 21)

Highlighting tape

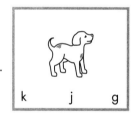

k   j   g

How to Play

1. Say the name of the picture slowly and listen for the ending or beginning sound, depending on which basket players are working with.

2. Place a piece of highlighting tape over the correct choice of ending or beginning sound. (Players can use the same piece of tape for the entire activity.)

3. Turn the card over to check the answer, reading the name of the object and its correct beginning or ending sound.

Note: For extra challenge, you can provide the initial and ending sounds as choices. This will help students discriminate between beginning and ending sounds.

Scholastic Teaching Resources © 2005

A a	B b	C c
D d	E e	F f
G g	H h	I i
J j	K k	L l

M m	N n	O o
P p	Q q	R r
S s	T t	U u
V v	W w	X x
Y y	Z z	

20 Reading and Writing Centers

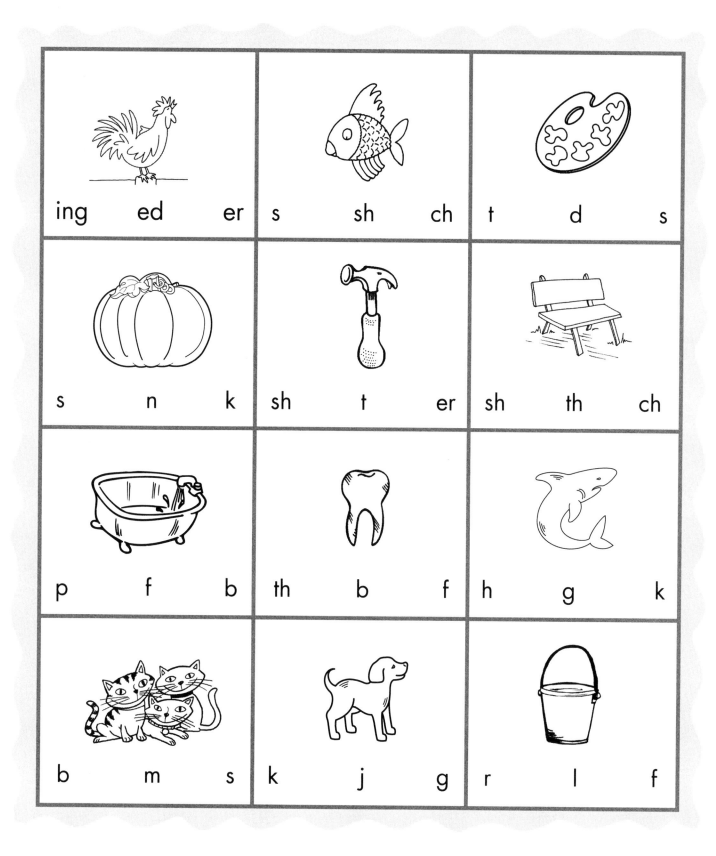

ing ed er	s sh ch	t d s
s n k	sh t er	sh th ch
p f b	th b f	h g k
b m s	k j g	r l f

CHAPTER 2

Word and Letter Recognition

It is essential for students to have a core of known words that they can read and write fluently. The centers in this chapter give children a variety of ways to practice reading and writing letters and high-frequency words, thereby building their bank of known words. When reading and writing a new text, students can easily recognize and write these words, which frees them up to problem-solve unknown words.

Station 6: Sticks, Dots, Circles, and Tunnels

To use at the beginning of the year

Skills Practiced
- Distinguishing distinct features of letters

Preparation
1. Make separate laminated task cards for each letter feature, using the templates on pages 27–28.
2. Print the letters that correspond to the heading on the back of each card.
3. Place the cards in a basket labeled "Sticks, Dots, Circles, and Tunnels." Model the procedure below before making the center available during center time.

Materials

A variety of upper- and lower-case magnetic letters in a sorting tray

Laminated cards made from the templates on pages 27–28

Letters by type

letters with sticks—A, a, B, b, D, d, E, F, H, h, I, i, K, k, L, l, M, N, P, p, R, r, T, t, Z, z

with slants—A, K, k, M, N, R, V, v, W, w, X, x, Y, y, Z, z

with tunnels—h, m, n, U, u

with dots—i, j

with hooks—f, g, J, j

with sticks and slants—A, K, k, M, N, W, w, Y, y, Z, z

with circles and sticks—a, B, b, d, P, p, Q, q

with sticks and tunnels—M, n, U, u

How to Play

1. Read the heading on the task card and find the appropriate magnetic letters that match the description. Place the letters on the task card.

2. Once the task card is completed, slide the letters off the card and turn the card over to check whether the magnetic letters match the letters on the back of the task card.

Station 7: Missing Letter Game

To use at the beginning of the year

Skills Practiced

- Developing fluency of alphabet sequence and letter formation

Preparation

1. Make six sets of cards. Begin with the cards on page 29, but create others as needed, using both lower- and upper-case letters. Two sets leave out the initial letter in a series of three alphabet letters (one set is upper case, one is lower case). Two sets leave out the middle letter in a series of three letters. The last two sets leave out the final letter in a series of three letters.

2. Write the missing letter on the back of each card.

3. Laminate cards, if desired.

4. Place the cards in a basket labeled "Missing Letter Game." Model the procedure below before making the center available to students.

How to Play *(in pairs or individually)*

1. Read the card and identify what letter is missing.

2. Choose the correct letter from the magnetic letter sorting tray.

3. Write the letter on a separate dry-erase board using a dry-erase marker.

4. Check the answer by turning over each card and looking at the correct letter on the back.

Station 8: Word Bingo

To use throughout the year

Skills Practiced

- Reading high-frequency words

Preparation

1. Create game boards by copying the template on page 18 onto construction paper or cardboard.

2. Use the words you're currently working on to fill in the boxes. (You may choose word wall words or high-frequency words, for example.) Write a word in each box in different order on each board. Each board should include a word or two that is different from those on the other boards.

3. Make separate word cards, each containing one word from the different game boards.

4. Place the game boards and word cards in a basket labeled "Word Bingo." Model the procedure below before making the center available to students.

Materials

Bingo game boards

- Template on page 18
- Construction paper or cardboard

Word cards

- Index cards
- Word wall words or high-frequency words

Bingo markers

How to Play *(in groups of two or three)*

1. Each player selects one bingo game board and bingo markers (six or nine markers depending on how many boxes are on the player's bingo card).

2. One player holds up a word card.

3. Players read the word and see if they have that word on their bingo card. If they do, they place a marker on the word.

4. When someone fills up his or her entire card, a new game begins.

Note: This station needs to be updated on an ongoing basis, adding new words as well as deleting words that children have mastered.

Station 9: Word Shape-Up Game

To use throughout the year

Skills Practiced

- Distinguishing and matching features of letters and words
- Reading high-frequency words

Preparation

1. Write high-frequency words on cardboard paper and cut out their shapes; see the sample at right.

2. On another piece of cardboard, outline the shape of each word that was just cut out and cut it out. You'll have shapes with words on them and shapes that are blank.

3. Put Velcro on the back of the word shape and on the front of the blank shape.

4. Place the cards in a basket labeled "Word Shape-Up Game." Model the procedure below before making the center available to students.

Materials

Shaped word cards (see samples on pages 30–31)

- Oaktag
- High-frequency word list

Shaped cards

- Cardboard
- Shaped word cards

Velcro

How to Play

Read each word and fit it into the correct shape.

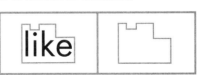

Station 10: Let's Go Fishing

To use throughout the year

Skills Practiced
- Reading and writing high-frequency words

Preparation
1. Trace and cut out 10 to 15 cardboard fish, using the template on page 32.
2. Write one high-frequency word on each fish.
3. Place a piece of magnetic tape on each fish and place it in a bowl or container.
4. To make a fishing rod, tie a large paper clip to the end of the string and attach the string to the end of the pencil.
5. Make copies of the Word Recording Sheet on page 32.
6. Place the fish, container, fishing pole, sorting tray and letters, and copies of the Word Recording Sheet in a basket labeled "Let's Go Fishing." Model the procedure below before making the center available to students.

Materials
Fish template (see page 32)

Cardboard paper

Small bowl or container

Magnetic tape

Unsharpened pencils

Pieces of string

Paper clips

Magnetic letters in a sorting tray

Word Recording Sheet (see page 32)

How to Play *(in pairs)*
1. One partner puts the fishing rod in the bowl, picks up a fish, and reads the word on it.
2. The other partner makes the word with magnetic letters.
3. Each of the partners keeps a written list on a separate sheet of paper of all the words they caught.

Station 11: Making and Breaking

To use throughout the year

Skills Practiced
- Reading and writing high-frequency words

Preparation
1. Put magnetic letters in a sorting tray with a separate compartment for each letter so that children don't have to spend time searching for letters.
2. Write on an index card each high-frequency word children have learned. (See pages 33–34 for some words to start with.)
3. On each library pocket card, one for each letter of the alphabet, write a lower- and upper-case letter.

Materials
Magnetic letters in a sorting tray

Index cards

26 library pocket cards

4 or 5 pieces of cardboard

Dry-erase board and marker

4. Glue the pocket cards to separate pieces of cardboard, eight to ten per piece. Put the word cards in the appropriate pocket ("went" in the "Ww" pocket, for example). Place finished pieces of cardboard in a folder for storage.

5. Place the storage folder in a basket labeled "Making and Breaking." Model the procedure below before making the center available to students.

Aa	Bb	Cc
Dd	Ee	Ff
Gg	Hh	Ii

How to Play
1. Take one word card out of the file folder.
2. Form the word using the magnetic letters.
3. Read the word again, running a finger underneath it to check whether it looks right.
4. Write the word on the dry-erase board.
5. Put word card back in its appropriate pocket.

Station 12: Look-Say-Name-Cover-Write-Check

(From a technique developed by Diane Snowball, *Spelling K–8: Planning and Teaching*, 1999)

To use in the middle and end of the year

Skills Practiced
• Reading and writing high-frequency words

Preparation
1. Prepare one index card for each high-frequency word the children have learned. (See pages 33–34 for a selection of high-frequency words.)
2. Copy the template on page 35 onto a piece of cardboard. Laminate it.
3. On each empty space on the template, place a piece of Velcro.
4. On the back of each word card place a piece of Velcro.
5. Place the cards and template in a basket labeled "Look-Say-Name-Cover-Write-Check." Model the procedure below before making the center available to students.

Materials
Index cards

Dry-erase marker

Laminated template (see page 35)

Velcro

How to Play
1. Take one word card and place it on the Velcro next to the word *look*.
2. Move it down to *say* and read the word.
3. Move it down again to *name* and name the letters of the word or clap and chant the word (Cunningham, 2000).
4. Move it down again to the word *cover*. Turn the card over so the word is covered.
5. Write the word next to the word *write* on the template.
6. Turn the card and check it against the written word.

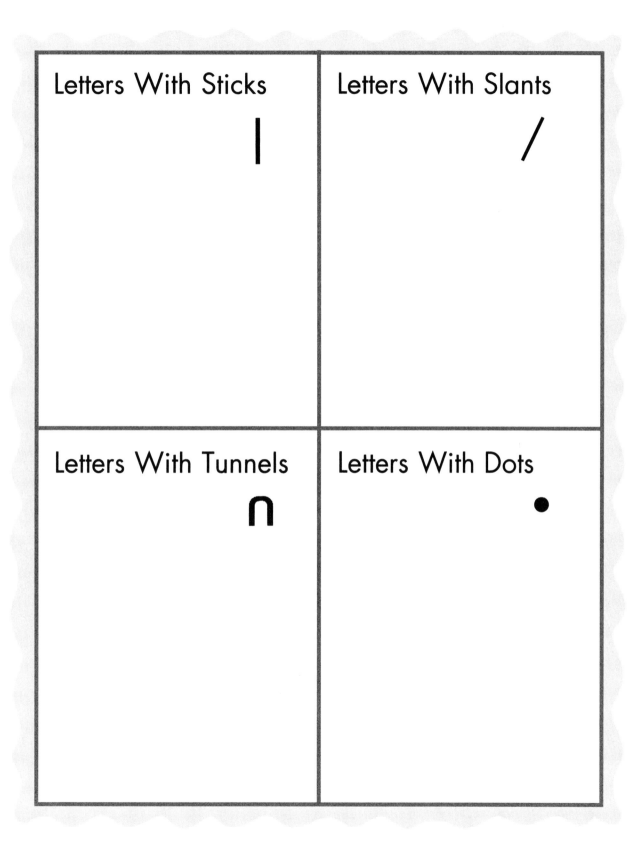

Letters With Sticks	Letters With Slants

Letters With Tunnels	Letters With Dots

Letters With Hooks J	Letters With Sticks and Slants I /
Letters With Circles and Sticks o l	Letters With Sticks and Tunnels I n

a b _	d e _	g h _
j k _	m n _	p q _
s t _	v w _	x y _
a _ c	d _ f	g _ i
j _ l	m _ o	p _ r
s _ u	v _ x	x _ z

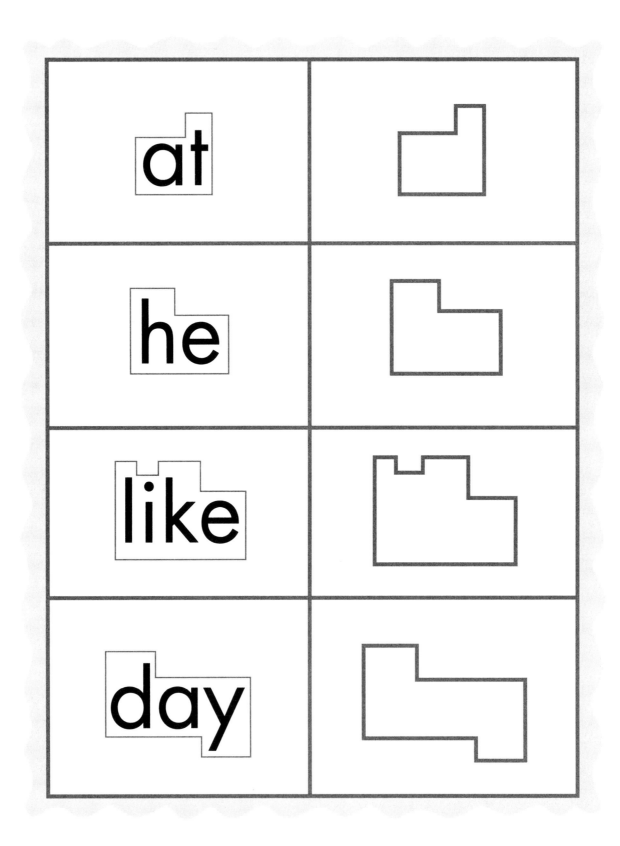

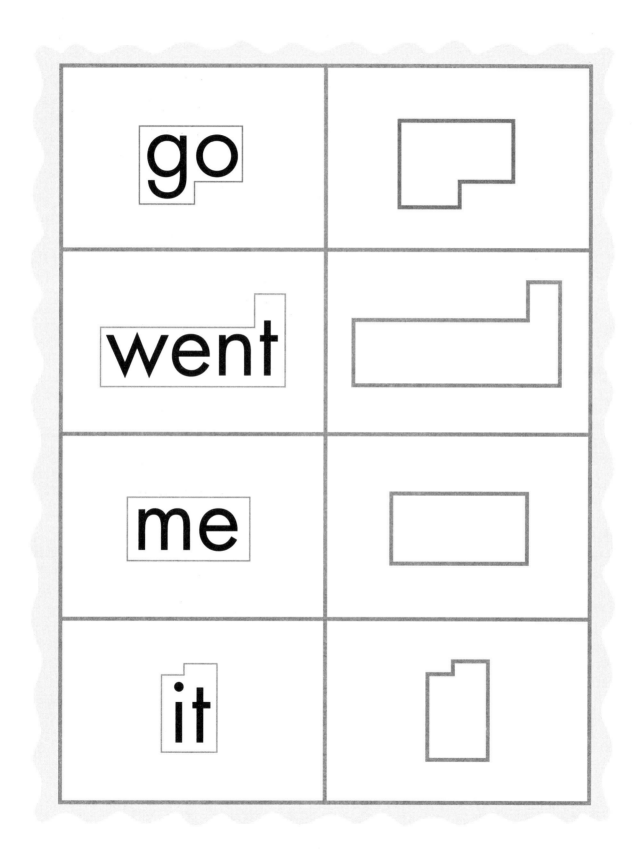

Name: _____

1. _____

2. _____

3. _____

4. _____

5. _____

6. _____

7. _____

8. _____

9. _____

10. _____

look	like	can
me	we	he
she	in	is
it	my	up

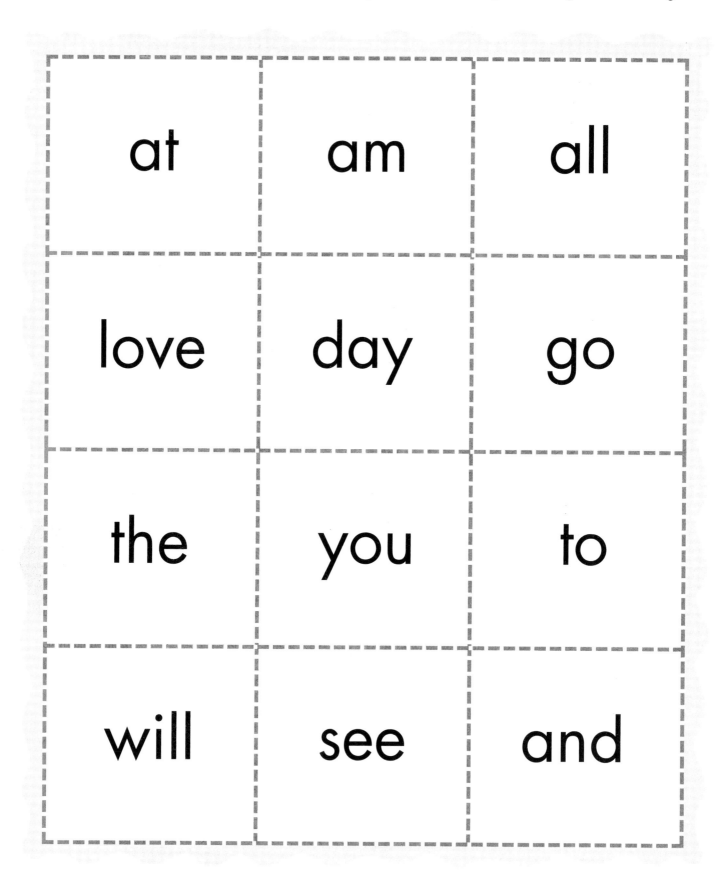

at	am	all
love	day	go
the	you	to
will	see	and

Look	
Say	
Name	
Cover	
Write	
Check	

20 Reading and Writing Centers   Scholastic Teaching Resources © 2005

CHAPTER 3

Word Study

Word study centers help children learn how to take words apart when reading and to put words together when writing by manipulating onsets and rimes, or chunks. Children begin to understand the concept that knowing one word can help them get to a new word. For example, if they are trying to write the word *stay* they can use the known word *day*. When they're reading, they will be able to recognize chunks in words and use this visual cue as a source of information to problem-solve new words.

Station 13: Word Sorting

To use at the middle and end of the year

Skills Practiced
- Sorting words according to their chunks
- Becoming familiar with known parts of words

Preparation

Materials
Index cards

Magnetic tape

Magnetic board

Sorting mat (see page 40)

1. Write one word on each of four cards and place a piece of magnetic tape on the back of each card. Choose words that contain specific chunks or rimes that you're working on with the class. Include words with two different chunks. For example, the words to sort are *like, look, bike, book, Mike, hike.*

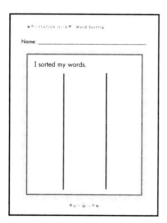

2. Make copies of the Sorting Mat Template on page 40; students will record their words here.

3. As the children begin to master the concept, include three categories of chunks to sort.

4. Place the magnetic word cards and copies of the sorting mat in a basket labeled "Word Sorting." Model the procedure below before making the center available to students.

How to Play

1. Categorize or sort the words on a magnetic board or the side of a file cabinet, according to their chunks.
2. After sorting the words, players write down the words in their separate categories on the word sorting template.

Station 14: Roll the Chunk

To use at the end of the year

Skills Practiced

- Forming new words from known words
- Integrating meaning, structure, and visual cue sources of information

Preparation

1. Place a sticky dot on each side of two cubes or dice. On one of the cubes, write the chunk you want your students to practice on each sticky dot.

2. On the other cube, write a different letter or letter combination on each sticky dot, which will form a word with the chunk from the other cube. For example, if the chunk written on one cube is *ook*, the letters written on the other cube might be *b* to create *book*, *l* to create *look*, *c* to create *cook*, or *sh* to create *shook*. (See page 38 for a list of chunks and onsets.)

3. For each set of cubes, prepare a sheet of paper with sentences that have a word missing; the missing words should all have the same chunk and can be created with the cubes. On the bottom corner of the paper, write the chunk that the sentences correspond to. Make a corresponding picture for each sentence. Laminate each sheet. (See models on pages 41–43.)

4. Place magnetic letters that correspond to the words created by the cubes in plastic bags.

5. Prepare an answer sheet for the missing words from the sentences for each set of cubes.

6. Place the cubes, magnetic letters, laminated sentence sheet, and answer sheet in a basket labeled "Roll the Chunk." If you want to make more than one chunk available at a time, place each set of materials in a labeled plastic bag, and store the bags in the basket. Model the procedure below before making the center available to students.

Note: You may have four different chunks using eight different cubes at this station at one time. However, keep each set of cubes separate from the others so that the children work with one set at a time.

Word Sorting Words

Suggested words for the Word Sorting Activity:

day, way, pay, say, away
will, hill, pill, sill, still
cow, now, how
cat, sat, bat, pat, chat
pin, win, tin, chin
ham, Sam, Pam
got, pot, lot, spot
get, let, set, pet
can, man, pan, Stan, fan
ring, wing, sing, sting
my, by, shy, try
sit, pit, lit, hit
ball, tall, call, fall, mall
went, tent, sent, rent
like, bike, hike, Mike
look, book, hook, shook

Materials

2 six-sided cubes or dice, 1" x 1" (use cubes from math manipulatives or word cubes)

Colored sticker dots

Dry-erase markers

Magnetic letters

Plastic bags

Sticky dots

Laminated sentence sheets (see pages 41–43 for models)

How to Play

1. Throw the two cubes or dice and read the word that the cubes make.

2. Use the magnetic letters to make the word.

3. Read the sentences from the sheet and look for the one sentence that fits the word.

4. Check to see whether the word makes sense in the sentence using meaning, structure, and visual cue sources of information ("Does it look right? Sound right? Make Sense?").

5. With a dry-erase pen, write the missing word on the laminated sentence sheet.

6. The other partner repeats the sequence.

7. When the sheet is filled, the partners check it against the answer sheet and erase the words before going on to the next set.

Note: If there are fewer than six onsets for a chunk, simply duplicate an onset. So for –ike, you could have l and b appear twice on the die, and write two different sentences for like and bike.

Sample Chunks and Companion Letters

in—p, t, f, b, w, ch
it—b, f, h, l, p, s
ill—w, h, p, b, s, st
ing—s, r, w, th
ike—l, b, m, h
ook—l, b, t, c, h, sh
op—h, m, c, t, sh, p
ot—d, g, n, h, p, sh
ow—n, c, h, w
at—s, p, h, th, c, b
an—m, t, v, c, p, f
ay—d, m, s, p, h, pl
all—b, c, t, h, f, m
et—g, m, l, s, b, n
en—p, h, t, b, d, th
ent—w, s, b, t, l, r

Station 15: Rhyme Time

To use in the middle and end of the year

Skills Practiced

- Hearing similar sounds in different words
- Understanding that words that rhyme or sound the same often have the same chunk
- Forming new words from known words

Preparation

1. Make multiple copies of a rhyming poem that you've read during Shared Reading. Leave space on the bottom of the page for children to write another word with the same chunk; see samples on pages 44–45.

2. Place the poem pages and highlighters in a basket labeled "Rhyme Time." Model the procedure below before making the center available to students.

How to Play

1. Read a copy of the poem.

2. Highlight all of the words that sound the same.

3. Write a new word with the same chunk at the bottom of the poem.

Materials

Highlighters

Copies of poems read during Shared Reading; see samples on pages 44–45

Station 16: What's the Word?

(Adapted from Patricia Cunningham and Richard Allington's *Classrooms That Work*, 1999.)

To use at the end of the year

This station requires a more sophisticated use of the chunking process and children need to be able to read unfamiliar sentences independently. This is not introduced as a station until this word study activity is practiced with the class.

Skills Practiced

- Forming new words from known words

Preparation

1. Make laminated task cards of the sentences on pages 46 and 47. Each sentence gives a written clue for a high-frequency word. For example, a written clue for the word *like* would be: "It starts like *ladder* and rhymes with *bike*." (*like*) Each sentence also has a picture next to the content words, such as *ladder* and *bike*. (You may wish to create your own sentences for words on your Word Wall for this activity.)

2. On the back of each task card, write the correct word.

3. Laminate each task card so that children can write on it.

4. Place the task cards in a basket labeled "What's the Word?" Model the procedure below before making the center available to students.

Materials

Task cards

Large index cards

Illustrated sentences (see pages 46–47)

Dry-erase markers

How to Play

1. Sit by the Word Wall or have a list of high-frequency words available.

2. Choose a card and find the correct word on the Word Wall or list.

3. Write the word on the card.

4. Turn the card over to check the answer.

Name: _____

I sorted my words.

–*an* Chunk

I _____ read books.

The _____ is hot.

The _____ is at the door.

The girl _____ in the park.

It is hot. Put on the _____.

My name is _____.

–ook Chunk

I like to _____ at birds.

I love to read a _____ in school.

I _____ my sister's toy.

I put my coat on the _____.

The leaves _____ on the trees.

I like to _____ soup.

–all Chunk

Do not _____ off the ladder.

The man is _____.

The mouse is _____.

I play with the _____.

The picture is on the _____.

I _____ my dog Spot.

Bill and Jill

My name is Bill.

I ran up a hill.

I saw my friend Jill.

Oh, what a thrill!

Write a new word that has the same chunk. _____

By R. Franzese and D. Rosen, and L. Golden

The Tent

I saw a big tent.

It was old, rusty, and really bent.

So I just stood up and went.

Write a new word that has the same chunk. _____

By L. Chasen

Kit

My name is Kit.

I want to sit.

I do not fit.

Please move over a bit.

Write a new word that has the same chunk. _____

By R. Franzese and D. Rosen, and L. Golden

Tall

I am tall.

I am not small.

I like to play ball.

Look out if I fall.

Write a new word that has the same chunk. _____

By S. Chasen

It starts like <u>goat</u> and rhymes with <u>pot</u>.

It starts like <u>ladder</u> and rhymes with <u>bike</u>.

It starts like <u>window</u> and rhymes with <u>tent</u>.

It starts like <u>mouse</u> and rhymes with <u>by</u>.

It starts like <u>ladder</u> and rhymes with <u>book</u>.

It starts like <u>horse</u> and rhymes with <u>me</u>.

It starts like <u>nest</u> and rhymes with <u>go</u>.

It starts like <u>bike</u> and rhymes with <u>my</u>.

It starts like <u>cat</u> and rhymes with <u>man</u>.

It starts like <u>window</u> and rhymes with <u>hill</u>.

It starts like <u>dog</u> and rhymes with <u>play</u>.

It starts like <u>nest</u> and rhymes with <u>got</u>.

It starts like <u>shoe</u> and rhymes with <u>me</u>.

It starts like <u>wheel</u> and rhymes with <u>then</u>.

CHAPTER 4

Comprehension and Fluency

These centers give children the opportunity to reread familiar texts in order to practice reading strategies and develop fluency. Students reread poems and texts in the centers that have been introduced during shared reading. As they reread, they are integrating meaning, structure, and visual cue sources of information. The centers also provide opportunities for children to monitor and check their comprehension. These centers help students pull together all the skills and strategies that they have learned and then apply them in a meaningful context.

Station 17: Missing Word Bingo

To use at the end of the year

Skills Practiced
- Integrating meaning, structure, and visual cueing sources of information
- Reading high-frequency words

Preparation
1. Make three or four game boards by dividing pieces of cardboard or poster board into four boxes.
2. In each box, write a sentence leaving out a high-frequency word. Replace the word with a line. Draw pictures to support the content words of the sentences; see samples on pages 52–53.
3. Prepare word cards for each of the missing words. You'll find word cards with high-frequency words on pages 33–34.
4. Place the game boards and word cards in a basket labeled "Missing Word Bingo." Model the procedure below before making the center available to students.

How to Play *(small groups of three or four)*
1. One player picks up a word card and reads the word.
2. The other players read through the sentences on their boards to see if they have the

> **Materials**
>
> Game boards
> - Posterboard or cardboard
> - Templates on pages 52–53
>
> Bingo markers
>
> Word cards (see pages 33–34)

sentence that the word fits into; the word has to make sense, sound right, and look right. If they do, they place the card over the sentence on the board.

3. Once a player completes his or her card, players choose another card and repeat the activity.

Station 18: Poetry Strips

To use throughout the year

Skills Practiced

- Sequencing text for meaning
- Integrating meaning, structure, and visual cue sources of information
- Reading high-frequency words
- Practicing fluency and phrasing

Materials

Large business-size envelopes

Sentence strips (see sample poems on pages 54–56)

Preparation

1. On the outside of an envelope, write each of the poems you've read during Shared Reading.

2. Write each poem on sentence strips, one line to a strip of paper. Draw a picture clue beside each line of the poem on both the outside of the envelope and on each sentence strip. Put the strips in the envelope.

3. Place each set of sentence strips in the appropriate envelope. Put a selection of envelopes in a basket labeled "Poetry Strips." Model the procedure below before making the center available to students.

Note: As the year progresses, you can make this station more challenging by cutting each line of the poem word by word.

How to Play

1. Read the poem.
2. Remake the poem with sentence strips.
3. Reread the poem to check and see if the text makes sense, sounds right, and looks right.

Station 19: Guess and Check

To use throughout the year

Skills Practiced

- Integrating meaning, structure, and visual cue sources of information

Materials

Magnetic tape

Plastic bags

Cardboard paper

Preparation

1. Write passages from familiar Big Books and poems from Shared Reading lessons on separate sheets of paper, replacing certain words with fill-in lines. Try to use only part of text from a Big

Book, since including the entire book can be overwhelming for kindergartners. However, do use entire poems because the familiarity of the rhythm or pattern helps children figure out the missing words. Several sample poems are provided on pages 54–56; corresponding sentence strips for activity are on pages 57–58.

2. Draw pictures next to certain words to help children read the text.

3. Put a strip of magnetic tape above each line.

4. Mount these sheets on cardboard or thick paper.

5. Write on a separate small card each word deleted from the passage.

6. Put a magnetic-tape strip on the back of each small card.

7. Make an answer key for each selection by writing the sentence with the answer filled in on a separate sheet of paper.

8. Keep everything for each passage or poem together in one plastic bag labeled "Guess and Check." Model the procedure below before making the center available to students.

How to Play

1. Read the passage and try to figure out the missing words.

2. Read the word cards and attach the appropriate word to the blank line with the magnetic tape.

3. Check work with the answer key.

Note: Every time you finish reading a Big Book or poem, add it to this station and take away any texts that you feel children have mastered.

Station 20: Book Making

To use throughout the year

Skills Practiced

- Developing one-to-one matching
- Integrating meaning, structure, and visual cue sources of information
- Developing fluency and phrasing

Preparation

1. Make copies of the pictures in the book.

2. Rewrite the text on separate sentence strips.

3. Mix up the pictures and sentence strips and put them in a plastic bag with the book. Label the bag "Book Making." Model the procedure below before making the center available to students.

Materials

Pocket chart

Smaller version of a familiar Big Book (sample provided on pages 59–61)

How to Play

1. Read the text on the strips and match them to their appropriate pictures.

2. Put the story back together in correct sequential order in a pocket chart, on a table, or on the floor.

3. Check work by rereading the book.

Station 21: Listening Center

To use throughout the year

Skills Practiced

- Developing one-to-one matching
- Developing comprehension; locating supportive evidence in the text
- Locating and framing high-frequency words
- Promoting meaning and use of punctuation marks
- Developing fluency and phrasing

Preparation

1. Tape-record your own version of the Big Books you are using in Shared Reading.

2. Read the story three times, giving directions right on the tape (see scenario below).

3. Label each tape with the book title and store it in its own plastic bag with the corresponding small version of the Big Book. Model the procedure below before making the center available to students.

4. Teacher-Recorded Big Book Reading

    First Reading: *I'm going to read the story first. You can follow along as I read it to you.* [Read story.]

    Second Reading: *This time, as I read the story, I want you to read along with me and point to the words.* [Read story.] After reading the story through the second time, ask children to answer comprehension questions based on the story by locating the evidence in the text: *Why did . . . ? What happened when . . . ? Talk to your partner about your answer and see if you can find it in the story.* Give them time to answer each question and then go over the answer with them, going back to the page in the text that supports the answer: *The answer is . . . . Let's turn to page xx and read it together.* You might ask the children to turn to a specific page and frame or locate a high-frequency word you've been working on or to locate a specific punctuation mark.

    Third Reading: *Let's read the story again together, and we'll practice smooth reading as if we were talking.* [Read story.] *Now turn the tape player off and read the story on your own or with your partner.*

5. After the students read the book, they do a written response. The written response sheets are introduced in the middle of the year. Each response sheet is modeled quite a few times before the children do it on their own. The types of response sheets are as follows: What was your favorite part of the book?, Who was your favorite character?, and Where did the story take place? are other types of response sheets.

How to Play

Listen to the tape and follow the instructions.

I _____ to
go to the park.

I _____ to
a fun school.

We _____
read books.

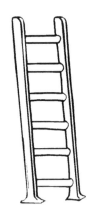

I go _____
the ladder.

I _____ so happy.

I _____ my family.

I like to _____ at the stars.

I like _____ eat bananas.

Feelings

I am so happy.

I am so mad.

I am so sad.

I am so glad.

I am me!

Poem by R. Franzese

What Can I Do?

I can jump.

I can run.

I can sing.

I can dance.

I can do so many things!

Poem by R. Franzese, D. Rosen, and L. Golden

This is Me!

This is my hair.

This is my nose.

This is my mouth.

This is my big toe.

This is me!

Poem by D. Rosen

The Sandwich

Take out the bread.

Take out the lettuce.

Take out the cheese.

Take out the ham.

Now I can make a sandwich!

Poem by D. Rosen

My Friend

She likes apples.

She likes grapes.

She likes strawberries.

On her cake.

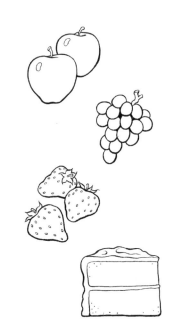

Poem by R. Franzese, D. Rosen, and L. Golden

Baby

The baby is laughing.

He is happy.

He is smiling at me.

We love the baby!

Poem by R. Franzese, D. Rosen, and L. Golden

Feelings

I ____ so happy.

I am ____ mad.

I am so sad.

____ am so glad.

I am ____!

Poem by R. Franzese

The Sandwich

Take out ____ bread.

Take ____ the lettuce.

Take out the cheese.

____ out the ham.

Now I ____ make a sandwich!

Poem by D. Rosen

This is Me!

This is _____ hair.

This _____ my nose.

_____ is my mouth.

This is _____ big toe.

This is _____!

Poem by D. Rosen

What Can I Do?

I _____ jump.

_____ can run.

I can _____.

I can dance.

I can _____ _____ many things!

Poem by R. Franzese, D. Rosen, and L. Golden

20 Reading and Writing Centers   Scholastic Teaching Resources © 2005

School

I see the book.

I see the paint.

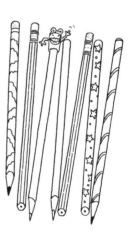

I see the pencils.

I see the lunchbox.

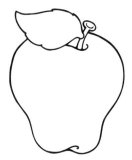

I see the apple.

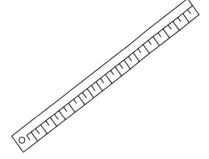

I see the ruler.

I see the bus.

I see the teacher.

I see the principal.

I see the children.

I love school!

Name: _____

Title: _____

What was your favorite part of the book?

Name: _____

Title: _____

Who was your favorite character?

Name: _____

Title: _____

Where did the story take place?

20 Reading and Writing Centers   Scholastic Teaching Resources © 2005